Creating Compassionate Children
A Character Development Program ™

A PROJECT OF UNICORN CHILDREN'S FOUNDATION

www.GetCaughtBeingKind.org

REVIEWS
Exceptionally Good Friends: Building Relationships with Autism

"*Exceptionally Good Friends* is a book with a great deal of information on autism. It is useful for parents, teachers, therapists, and children of all ages."
> – Nancy Kashman, Occupational Therapist, *Co-author of The Sensory Connection, An OT and SLP Team Approach*

"Melissa Burkhardt presents the story of Clay, a boy who has autism, from his own perspective and also from the perspective of a typically developing girl in his class. This creative approach lets children see Clay's behavior in a positive light from the outside while also giving them a window into Clay's own perceptions and experiences. The stories are engaging in their own right, but they are made even more valuable by the extensive resources Mrs. Burkhardt offers for both teachers and parents, all of which are linked very helpfully to specific episodes in the stories. Teachers, therapists, and parents alike will find this book to be an invaluable and practical resource."
> – Kathleen M. Cain, Ph.D., Associate Professor of Psychology, Gettysburg College

"*Exceptionally Good Friends: Building Relationships with Autism* does an excellent job of presenting Asperger's and children with autism as unique with their own sets of strengths and weaknesses. The book presents their integration into the regular classroom setting as a very natural thing and provides much information for teachers or paraprofessionals to use in adapting the approach or environment. The book would make a great interactive tool to share with a child, and the style makes it easy to do so."
> – Alan L. Taylor, Ph.D., Clinical Psychologist

"As an elementary school principal with a sincere fondness for children with special needs, I find this book to be one of the most valuable resources for any school, parent, or faculty. It is a true look into the experiences of a child with autism in an elementary school. The ideas and practices expressed in this book are written for the beginner as well as the experienced teacher. Parents will find it comforting and user friendly. Most importantly, it is evident to me that this book was written with a genuine love for children with autism and those who have the awesome opportunity of teaching or raising these truly gifted children. Finally, a book that is a 'real' teaching tool!"
> – Lauren Spencer, M.Ed., Elementary School Principal, Adjunct Professor of Education, Southeastern Louisiana University

"I absolutely love the book!!! I must admit it made me cry a little. I wish all kids were as sensitive to the needs of others...all kids should read this book."
> – Ashley B.-parent of a child with autism

"This is a must have for every early childhood classroom.…The story takes you on a journey from two different perspectives in a very unique way providing true insight into the everyday life of a child on the autism spectrum. The book also gives useful nuggets of advice and resources that teachers can utilize within their classroom and parents can utilize at home. And last but not least, the book shows the beautiful friendships that can develop within inclusive educational settings."

    – Shelley Nowicki, Mother of a child on the Autism Spectrum, Educator, Advocate and Parent liaison for Strengthening Outcomes with Autism Resources (soar)

"*Exceptionally Good Friends: Building Relationships with Autism* is an easy-to-read, yet very informative book, about those on the autism spectrum. Because it is written from two different points of view…that of the typically developing child and the one with ASD…it strikes a chord with everyone who reads it. The parent, teacher, relative, therapist, and child will have a better understanding of all who live in this beautiful world of ours, as varied as it is and as challenging as it can be. This book will help to build understanding and empathy for those whose lives are touched by ASD. The resources made available in Ms. Burkhardt's book give each reader the power to grow as much as desired by that individual."

    – Paula Belou, Speech Language Pathologist

"I have never seen anything written in terms of the perspective of children with autism and what they're thinking, but it's an excellent way of explaining the differences between neurotypical children and children with autism so that there is an understanding of the actual differences. It's so easy for many children and adults as well to be confused by the reactions (or non-reactions) of autistic children. Your book is an excellent source to help guide those who want to increase their knowledge in the area of autism."

    – Anne C.-parent of a child with autism

"Mrs. Burkhardt was my child's Early Intervention teacher when he was 3 years old. When our son was in Mrs. Burkhardt's classroom, he had significant behavior problems. She will never know the magnitude of difference and influence she had in our lives. She helped my son tremendously and educated us as parents on how to fight for his rights in school and beyond. He is now 18 years old and attending a university in a program designed for students with autism spectrum disorder to help them achieve a life of opportunity, independence and success. He is also playing in a rock band. How things have changed from a child that could not take loud music, people, etc. to a one amp sound—loud! There is not a day that goes by that I do not say a prayer of thanks for having Mrs. Burkhardt as my child's teacher."

    – Lisa C.-parent of a young adult with autism

Exceptionally Good Friends

:Building Relationships with Autism

Ruthie's Story

Book I

By

Melissa K. Burkhardt, M.S. Ed., BCBA

Illustrated by Toby Mikle

Executive Publishing Company

DEDICATION

I dedicate this book to the children whom I have had the honor to teach and who have taught me something valuable every single day. I also dedicate this book to their families, who have shared their precious children with me and who never give up the fight to help their child reach their maximum potential.

"For I know the plans I have for you," declares the Lord, "plans to prosper you and not to harm you, plans to give you hope and a future." Jeremiah 29:11, NIV®

ACKNOWLEDGMENTS

I wish to express my deep gratitude for the love, tireless support, and encouragement of my beloved husband and best friend, Byron, whose contributions and input were priceless in my creation of this work. I am deeply grateful for the love and support of my father, who greatly values education and has always encouraged me to persevere. I am grateful for the love of my mother and my in-laws and for their enthusiasm about this project.

I would not have the knowledge or skills I have today without all of my wise mentors: Sarah Al-Juraid, Dr. Becky Bailey, Elizabeth Duncan, LaTanya Haynes, Nancy Kashman, Janet Mora, Shelley Nowicki, and Lauren Spencer, who have shared their knowledge with me and who have taken the time and energy to encourage and guide me on my journey. Thank you to Pennington Biomedical Research Center, Baton Rouge, Louisiana, for reviewing my book and for input on exercise for children. Thank you to Dr. Sheryl Rosin for assistance with the DSM-5 update. Many thanks to my talented illustrator, Toby Mikle, my graphics designer, Brad Brett, CGC Design, to Maria Burkhardt for editing assistance, and to my publisher. All of you are a blessing in my life.

INTRODUCTION
Exceptionally Good Friends: Building Relationships with Autism

The Introduction contains valuable information for understanding the concept of this book.

If you do not personally know someone with autism spectrum disorder (ASD), or know a family that is being touched by a child with ASD, statistics indicate that you probably will soon. ASD refers to a complex group of developmental disorders of the brain. Symptoms appear before age three and reflect delayed or abnormal development in language, social skills, and repetitive or restricted behavior. According to a study released in March 2014 by the Centers for Disease Control and Prevention (CDC), 1 in every 68 children has been identified with ASD. This new estimate is roughly 30 percent higher than previous estimates reported in 2012 of 1 in 88 children with ASD, a significant increase in number. The data continue to show that ASD is almost five times more common among boys than girls: 1 in 42 boys versus 1 in 189 girls. White children are more likely to be identified with ASD than are black and Hispanic children, possibly due to lack of awareness and screening.

The CDC report also shows that most children with ASD are diagnosed after age four, although ASD can be diagnosed as early as age two. Research has shown that early detection and intervention are the most powerful tools in helping children with ASD to reach their greatest potential. If you suspect your child may have ASD, or a developmental delay, you can ask your pediatrician for a screening. If your child is under the age of three, you can call 1-800-CDC-INFO to find the phone number for your state's early intervention program, or visit www.cdc.gov/Concerned. If your child is age three or older, contact your local elementary school and ask to speak to someone about having your child evaluated— even if your child does not go to that school. Your child may be eligible for early intervention services at no charge.

In May 2013, the American Psychiatric Association (APA) released the fifth edition of the *Diagnostic and Statistical Manual of Mental Disorders* (DSM-5), which contains new criteria for the diagnosis of ASD. This new criteria removes several diagnoses from the previous

DSM-IV, including Asperger's Syndrome and Pervasive Developmental Disorder-Not Otherwise Specified (PDD-NOS), and puts them on a continuum of autism spectrum disorder. Children diagnosed with ASD are now diagnosed ranging from mildly affected to severely affected. For children to meet the new and more stringent criteria for ASD under DSM-5, they must demonstrate weakness in social communication and have, or have had, restricted interests and repetitive behavior.

Children who would have been previously diagnosed as having Asperger's Syndrome or PDD-NOS may be diagnosed under the new DSM-5 criteria as having mild autism, or may not be diagnosed on the autism spectrum at all. These children may be diagnosed as having a new DSM-5 diagnosis, Social Communication Disorder. The possibility that children could lose services, or not receive needed services under the DSM-5 criteria, is a concern that has been expressed by parents and various autism advocacy groups. The new DSM-5 includes a statement specifying that individuals with a well-established DSM-IV diagnosis of autistic disorder, Asperger's Syndrome, or PDD-NOS should be given the diagnosis of autism spectrum disorder.

It is important to realize that children with ASD are all very unique and have an extremely wide range of functioning levels. Mildly affected children may have average to above-average academic skills but lack social reciprocity and are unable to have developmentally appropriate relationships. They are often experts on one subject and may only want to speak about this subject despite the obvious disinterest of others. Conversely, severely affected children may have little-to-no functional language, other developmental delays, and few social skills. They often have severe sensory processing disorder (SPD) resulting in repetitive, intense behaviors.

Early Red Flags & Signs of Autism

- By 6 months: No big smiles or other warm, joyful expressions
- By 9 months: No back-and-forth sharing of sounds, smiles, or other facial expressions
- By 12 months: No back-and-forth gestures, such as pointing, showing, reaching, or waving; lack of response to name; and, no babbling or "baby talk"
- By 16 months: No spoken words
- By 18 months: No play of "pretend" games (pretend to "feed" a doll)
- By 24 months: No meaningful two-word phrases that do not involve imitating or repeating
- At any age, any loss of: speech, babbling, or social skills

A person with ASD might:

- Avoid eye contact and want to be alone
- Have trouble understanding other people's feelings, or talking about their own feelings
- Have delayed speech and language skills
- Repeat words or phrases over and over (echolalia)
- Give unrelated answers to questions
- Get upset by minor changes
- Have obsessive interests
- Flap their hands, rock their body, or spin in circles
- Have unusual reactions to the way things sound, smell, taste, look, or feel

Reference – www.cdc.gov/ncbddd/autism/signs.html

Characters in this book are two wonderful children who become friends in their inclusive early childhood classroom. The story is told through the perspective of Ruthie, a young girl who is developing typically (neurotypical) and through Clay, a Hispanic boy with autism.

This book was written in response to a growing need I saw in society to help someone who may know little or nothing about autism spectrum disorder to gain understanding about ASD, as well as to assist both regular and special education teachers in meeting the needs of the increasing numbers of children with ASD now being placed in their classes. This book is intended to teach children and adults tolerance, empathy, and understanding—thus helping to reduce bullying. This book is also intended to furnish teachers (both regular and special education), therapists, parents and relatives practical, easy-to-implement ideas and resources to help children with autism spectrum disorder to experience success. The information in this book can be used with a wide range of developmental ages. Additional resource information for adults is included after *Clay's Story*.

ABOUT THE AUTHOR

Melissa K. Burkhardt, M.S. Ed., BCBA, earned her Board Certified Behavior Analyst (BCBA) certification in 2014, after completing requirements consisting of 1500 hours of supervised training, post-baccalaureate coursework, and passing the BCBA examination for certification. She has a post-baccalaureate certification in Behavior Intervention in Autism. As of 2015, Melissa is one of 150 certified Early Start Denver Model (ESDM) providers worldwide, trained in a therapy specifically designed for 12-48 month old children diagnosed with autism. She has earned over 50 graduate hours in addition to her Master of Science in Education degree. Melissa is a certified Floortime Provider (a core deficit intervention for autism). She is a Reading Specialist, specialized in dyslexia and teaching children with autism to read. As a certified Special Education Early Intervention Teacher, she taught in the public school system for 20 years and worked extensively along with Occupational Therapists, Speech and Language Pathologists, and family members, helping children with ASD to reach their greatest potential. She helped to pioneer public, full inclusion pre-K classes in her school county. She also completed all of the curriculum classes for the Montessori World Education Institute pre-primary certification.

Melissa specializes in private therapy providing very early intervention for children with autism and parental training to achieve best outcomes in a child's life. She shares her extensive knowledge about autism through public speaking, coaching, program development, and preparing specialized presentations for individuals, groups, and corporations. She serves as a consultant in the formulation of an autism insurance plan for a national company. Her undergraduate degree was completed at Louisiana State University in Baton Rouge, Louisiana. She attended graduate school and earned a Master of Science in Education degree from Loyola University in New Orleans, Louisiana. She has served as a Court Appointed Special Advocate (CASA) volunteer for abused and neglected children for over ten years.

Melissa has learned from experience that early intervention takes advantage of the brain's neural plasticity and is essential in helping a child with autism spectrum disorder to achieve success in developing to their full capacity.

❖ ❖ ❖

My name is Ruthie, and a new boy started school today. His name is Clay. Guess what? He is the cutest little boy I have ever seen! He seems so scared. He doesn't talk. The sweet little guy just cries, and hums really loudly, and flaps his hands. Mrs. Hope reminds us that even though everybody is different, we can all still be exceptionally good friends.

The whole class welcomes him to our school family by singing a special welcome song, "Welcome to our Class." Oh, no! He covers his ears and frowns. Maybe the music hurts his ears.

Mrs. Hope goes over our class rules by showing us pictures of children playing together, sharing, picking up their work, and more. Next, she shows Clay our schedule for the whole day. Clay looks at each picture as Mrs. Hope explains each part of our school day. We all love to talk about our schedule. I feel safe and happy knowing what will happen each day!

Every morning, we get to exercise! Mrs. Hope says, "Exercise gets our brains and bodies ready to learn, and it makes us healthy and super strong!" I can pull a friend in a wagon; I can ride a bicycle or a scooter; I can hop on a hippity hop; or I can do jumping jacks or windmills with my friends. Yay! I choose a blue scooter and zoom around.

Clay chases me – he likes me! Mrs. Hope tries to get Clay to hop like a frog on the yellow hippity hop. He pulls away from her, screams, and cries. I wonder, has he ever seen a hippity hop before today? I grab the red hippity hop, my favorite, and face Clay, bouncing like a kangaroo. "Like this, Clay, one, two, three." Clay's face lights up with a smile. He sits on the hippity hop just like me. "Yay, Clay!" He counts; I can hear him. He can count all the way up to 25. What a smart boy he is! I think I want to hop and count with my new friend every day at exercise time.

Every day, at center time, Clay chooses the train center. He lines up the cars with the engine first, caboose last, and the blue and white cars in between. The same way every day! He is cool like that! I count his trains, and he counts with me. He is the best counter ever! At first, he would yell and grab a train from me.

Mrs. Hope wrote a special story about Clay sharing his trains and read it to him. He loves to look at the story and the picture of him and me with the trains. He is getting much better at sharing. The special story Mrs. Hope wrote for Clay really helped!

Recess is my favorite! I love to play chase with my friends! We all take turns going super fast down the big slide. Zoom! Clay loves to pick up little rocks and drop them down the drain the whole recess time. Every day, I run by him and call his name. He acts like I am invisible. Sometimes, he watches all of his friends run by, but he never chases us or slides down the slides.

Today, we got a cool new bouncy car to play on at recess. We take turns acting like we are driving all of our friends to Disney World. We all call Clay to come ride with us. He walks over and watches us bounce up and down. He flaps his hands, and he smiles, so cute! Guess what? He climbs on and bounces with us!

It is autumn now, and Clay bounces with me every day. He chased me all around the playground today. He threw the colorful leaves in the air and laughed and laughed.

At snack time, Clay just sits at the table and cries. Could my friend be hungry? Mrs. Hope holds up pictures of two choices for snack – fish crackers or apple slices. Clay just cries. I wish Mrs. Hope would just give him both, but I know she is trying to get him to use his words. She holds up a picture of fish crackers and says, "I want fish crackers, please." She gives Clay three, and he eats them up.

For weeks now, Mrs. Hope has been giving Clay choices at snack time. Guess what happened today? Clay said, "I want apples, please." He gets four apple slices from Mrs. Hope. We are happy that our friend used his words. We all cheer for our friend!

I love to learn new things! This week, we are learning about our five senses. Wow! I hear with my ears, smell with my nose, taste with my mouth, see with my green eyes, and touch and feel with my hands. Mrs. Hope tells us that some people's senses work differently. Some people might need to wear glasses to see better. Some people cannot hear well, so they can tell what people are saying by looking at their lips or by sign language.

Mrs. Hope explained that some people have super-sensitive senses. Lights may hurt their eyes, or everyday sounds may hurt their ears. I bet that is why Clay always covers his ears and squints his eyes!

She told us that some people do not like the feel of sand or paint because their sense of touch is so sensitive. Some people's sense of taste works too well. Some food can taste really strong, like an onion. Yuck! I bet that is why Clay only eats bread, goldfish crackers, or apples. I don't like it when my shirt has a scratchy tag – I always make Mommy take it out. I guess my sense of touch is too sensitive, too!

We all have five senses, but everybody is a little different in how our five senses work. Now when I see someone who looks or acts differently, I will remember to be kind to them. Hooray, for our five senses!

We check our schedule; time to go home. Mrs. Hope walks Clay to his bus. He pulls his hand away and runs to me. Clay uses his words! "Bye-bye Ruthie, bye-bye Ruthie." He keeps saying it over and over, but he does not look at my face. He gives me a big hug and smiles his cutest smile. He made my day again! Mrs. Hope was right. Clay is an exceptionally good friend!

The End
of
Ruthie's Story
Book I

Flip Book Over

for

Clay's Story

Book II

and

Resource List for Adults

Flip Book Over

for

Ruthie's Story

Book I

Exceptionally Good Friends

Building Relationships with Autism

Clay's Story, A Boy with Autism

Book II

By

Melissa K. Burkhardt, M.S. Ed., BCBA

Illustrated by Toby Mikle

Executive Publishing Company

Oh, no! Mommy tells me, "A new school today, Clay, new friends." What is happening? Who are all these people? I hope they are nice to me. Where is Mommy going? I see my name on the floor where Mrs. Hope points. I stand on it. Music, I love music, if it is just right. This music is too loud; it makes my ears pound and hurt. I cover them and scream. Mrs. Hope turns it down. Just-right music makes my heart beat slowly, makes me smile. I hum and spin in a circle. The children all sing, "Welcome to our Class," and wave, and smile.

The just-right song is over. All the children sit on their names. I kneel and keep humming and swaying. Mrs. Hope holds up a picture of children sitting in a circle with their legs crossed. I love pictures. My mind is full of pictures. I make my legs cross just like the picture.

Mrs. Hope shows us all of the things we will do today. I do not understand all of her words, but I can understand a lot from the pictures. I keep checking my picture schedule. I need to know what will happen next to feel safe.

A little girl zooms by on a blue scooter. I stretch out my wings, make my special sounds from *Toy Story*, and chase after her. Zoom, zoom! I love to see the wheels turn and turn, round and round. Mrs. Hope takes me by my hand and shows me a picture of a big ball. I fall to the ground and start to cry and scream.

Wheels are turning! I have to look at the wheels! Mrs. Hope tries to get me to sit on the yellow ball. No, ouch, it will hurt me! The girl on the blue scooter gets a red ball and sits on it right in front of me. She bounces and counts, "One, two, three." Counting makes my heartbeat slow down. I sit on the yellow ball and bounce and count just like the girl. The bouncing and counting make me feel good, almost like the just-right music does.

Trains, trains, all in a row. First, the big red engine; next, the passenger trains; last, the caboose. Sixteen trains, all in a row. I lie down, so that I can see all the wheels turning, and I smile. My heart is just right. Another boy takes my passenger train. Why did he take it? I scream! Has to be 16 trains, 16 trains, has to be 16 trains!

Mrs. Hope shows me a story about me. The story shows me that friends like trains, too, and that they like it when I share. The story says that I can count out trains and give my friend eight, or Mrs. Hope can set the big timer. When all the time is gone, then it is my friend's turn with the trains. I really do not want to share, but I choose for Mrs. Hope to set the timer anyway.

My schedule says it is recess time. I search the ground for small rocks to drop down the drain. I love the plop, plop, plop, of the rocks as they disappear. I feel calm when I do this. Children run by. I look at them from the corners of my eyes and keep dropping rocks. I see something new – a big car that bounces on springs. I love to bounce!

I hear the children yell my name. I am scared, but I need to bounce, too. Hey, bouncing is fun! I smile, and my friends laugh and smile back. Ruthie jumps off the big car and runs.

I follow her up the slide and down. That felt great! I still like to drop rocks down the drain, but I like to chase my friends, too. They laugh and laugh when I make loud, silly noises, and I laugh, too! The kids are so nice to me. I feel happy at my new school!

Every day, Mrs. Hope has all of the children choose work off the shelf. There are always new, fun things to do. Sometimes, I do not want to work. Mrs. Hope says, "First, do this work, and then you get to choose." She shows me pictures of the work I have to do and then a picture of my very favorite thing, trains. I do my work, so that I can play with trains.

I string beads: red, yellow, red, yellow. I sort pom poms with tongs. I mix colors with an eyedropper. I use pop beads to make a necklace or write letters and shapes in the sand tray. Mrs. Hope always says this makes our hands strong, so that we can be great writers. I want to write my name!

Today, the classroom is too loud, too bright, and too busy for me. I feel scared and achy. I cover my ears. Mrs. Hope leads me to the Safe Center. I see pictures of faces frowning, laughing, and crying. I pick the frown face and hold it. I put a heavy blanket on my lap. I take deep breaths and blow on a windmill. I put headphones on my ears to block out the sounds of the class.

I feel better; my heartbeat slows down. I put the sad face away. I leave the headphones on, but now I am ready to finish the puzzle I was working on.

More words are coming out of my mouth. I hear the other children and love to repeat exactly what they say. I like to carry around a book Mrs. Hope made with pictures of all the different things I like. I look at the pictures and can say the words easier. I get so mad when I cannot tell someone what I want. Sometimes, I fall down and scream and kick!

Why don't they know what I want? I wish there were a picture in my book for everything in my head that I do not have words for.

My schedule says it is time to go home. Mrs. Hope holds my hand and walks me to the bus. Ruthie is walking away. I pull away from Mrs. Hope. I have to tell Ruthie, my very best friend, good-bye. I hug her; big hugs feel so good sometimes. "Bye-bye Ruthie, bye-bye Ruthie, bye-bye Ruthie." I am ready to go home now.

The End
of
Clay's Story
Book II

RESOURCE LIST FOR ADULTS
Practical Tips for Teachers, Therapists, and Parents

The listed websites are only a sample of the many helpful websites and resources available on autism spectrum disorder (ASD). Internet addresses in this book are accurate at the time of publication. Visit my website **www.ExceptionallyGoodFriends.com** to find a list of websites, resources on ASD, and discussion questions to help build empathy and understanding in children. Page numbers in this Resource List refer to pages in *Clay's Story*.

❀ *Clay's Story*, **Pages 2-3:** Schedules are an evidence-based practice that can help to reduce anxiety and related behaviors in children with ASD. A posted visual routine or an individual schedule provides a child with the gift of being prepared emotionally and mentally for what their day will bring both at home and at school. Children with ASD, and most young children, benefit from the use of visuals to promote language understanding. Visual social cue cards and posted visual rules empower children to make appropriate social choices.

www.nationalautismcenter.org/pdf/nac_parent_manual.pdf (for parents)

www.nationalautismcenter.org/pdf/NAC%20Ed%20Manual_FINAL.pdf (for schools) – These information-packed, free handbooks identify 11 evidence-based practices that have been thoroughly researched and have sufficient evidence to state that they are effective for use with children on the autism spectrum. Many of these evidence-based practices are featured in the Resource List in this publication, *Exceptionally Good Friends: Building Relationships with Autism*.

www.consciousdiscipline.com – "Shubert's Picture Rule Cards™" and "Daily Routine Cards®"—for school. "Routine and Responsibility Cards™"—for home. This site also offers music CDs for helping children build social connections. The music CD, "It Starts in the Heart," by Dr. Becky Bailey and Mr. Al, includes the song, "Welcome to our Class." This website helps a child to learn emotional self-regulation skills and it includes information targeted for children on the autism spectrum.

Activity Schedules for Children with Autism: Teaching Independent Behavior by L. E. McClannahan & P. J. Krantz - This book explains in detail how to teach a child with ASD to follow an activity schedule, both at home and at school, thus promoting independence.

www.mayer-johnson.com – "Boardmaker®" software is a design program to make and adapt curriculum materials and to create picture schedules and communication choice boards.

www.pecs.com – "Picture Exchange Communication System™" helps children with little-to-no verbal language learn to communicate by using pictures. This website can help to locate a training program or a trained speech therapist in your area. "Pics for PECS™" is a software program that can be used to make communication choice boards and schedules for children.

www.do2learn.com – This website offers free, printable visuals that can be used to make schedules. There is a fee to gain access to all of the pictures. It is very user-friendly.

Thinking in Pictures by Dr. Temple Grandin – Dr. Grandin is a person with autism who is a world-renowned autism activist, author, and speaker. She provides valuable insight into how a mind with autism works.

❀ *Clay's Story*, Pages 4-5: Children with ASD often have sensory processing disorder (SPD). This disorder can also affect children who are typically developing in all other areas, or it can go hand-in-hand with other learning disorders. Sensory processing disorder can be difficult to understand if you have not experienced it firsthand. Children with SPD process information through their senses and their muscles and vestibular sense (balance). The difficulty occurs as the information is being brought to the brain to process. Along the way, information can get lost, slowed down or sped up, or processed by the wrong part of the brain. It can be likened to driving a malfunctioning car that stops when you press the gas or speeds up when you blow the horn. Children with SPD can exhibit many unique, baffling behaviors, such as running into objects and people, feeling no sense of pain, and needing to move constantly. It is crucial not to judge a child's behavior as bad or purposeful. Taking the time to learn about a child's specific sensory needs can assist the child in adjusting to various situations.

Children on the autism spectrum, and all young children, greatly benefit from a daily sensory exercise time as well as sensory breaks throughout the day. Pennington Biomedical Research Center in Baton Rouge, Louisiana, recommends that children have 60 minutes (two 30-minute sessions or one 60-minute session) of exercise daily for optimal health. Sensory activities can be alerting or calming. No special equipment is needed. Jumping can give a child the joint compression they crave and help to improve alertness in a child. Hold the child's hands and count together as he or she jumps. Do windmills, jumping jacks, or wheelbarrow walk; jump on a mini trampoline, or swing. For deep calming

pressure, parents can put pillows on their child's back. A teacher can instruct children to line up or transition, by hopping like a bunny or crawling like a bug. Be a sensory detective; what may be calming for a child one day may overstimulate them another day. A qualified Occupational Therapist can evaluate a child and help to design a sensory diet for the child's needs.

Sensory exercise time is a great opportunity for social interaction and building social language. Children whose sensory needs are met are often more receptive to a peer's interactions. Children can get a heavy sensory workout by pulling a friend in a wagon or get vestibular input by having a friend pull. Most children are calmer, more focused, and ready to learn after a planned sensory exercise time.

www.sensory-processing-disorder.com – This website explains sensory processing disorder and has sensory products for purchase. It also has checklists for symptoms of SPD.

www.spdfoundation.net – This website has many free articles on sensory processing disorder. It also has a nationwide list of parent connection groups and free, online courses on SPD.

www.abilitations.com – This website contains sensory, learning, and behavioral solutions for purchase.

www.fhautism.com and **www.sensoryworld.com** – Websites of Future Horizons, Inc. contain many publications and resources for ASD and sensory processing disorder.

The Sensory Connection, An OT and SLP Team Approach by Nancy Kashman, OT, and Janet Mora, SLP.

The Out of Sync Child: Recognizing and Coping with Sensory Processing Disorder by Carol Kranowitz, M.A.

Building Bridges Through Sensory Integration by Paula Aquilla BSC, OT, Ellen Yack, Esc, Med, OT, and Shirley Sutton, BSC, OT.

About Sensory Integration: Forms, Checklists, and Practical Tools for Teachers and Parents by Carol Kranowitz, M.A., Stacey Szklut, Lynn Balzer-Martin, Elizabeth Haber and Deanna Iris Sava.

28 Instant Songames: Fun-Filled Activities for Kids 3-8 by Barbara Sher, MS, OTR.

✿ *Clay's Story*, **Pages 6-7**: The use of social narratives with children on the autism spectrum is an evidence-based practice. Children with ASD have difficulty understanding social perspectives of others. Social narratives are personalized stories that can give a child specific strategies and information about a difficult social situation, skill, or concept and can help to increase their skills in the area of understanding social perspectives. Carol Gray created Social Stories™, the most widely known of social narratives. Social narratives are very effective, easy to write, and can affect a child's behavior in a positive manner. They can be written for various subjects, such as sharing with a friend, raising a hand at school, or going to the doctor. A visual timer provides a child with an easy-to-understand visual limit. Timers can be used for sharing toys, counting down for transitions, and so forth. Children often see the timer, not the adult, as the limit setter. This can significantly cut down on power struggles.

www.thegraycenter.org – This site gives information about "Social Stories™" created by Carol Gray, and it also has resources.

The New Social Story Book by Carol Gray. **Comic Strip Conversations** by Carol Gray.

www.speakingofspeech.com – This site contains free, ready-made social narratives.

www.difflearn.com – Different Roads to Learning offers for purchase a wide range of autism toys, games, and learning aides.

www.lakeshorelearning.com – "Time Timer®," a large visual timer for use at home or school, is available for purchase at this website. Distinctive, high-quality products are also available to help promote a child's development in all domains.

❄ *Clay's Story*, **Pages 6-7 (continued):** Joint attention intervention and naturalistic teaching strategies are both evidence-based practices. Children with autism spectrum disorder have restricted interests and engage in repetitive play and behavior. Utilizing a child's intense interests can help to develop a child's joint attention, leading to the building of social language and social connections. Intense interests can be powerful motivators and reinforcers in naturalistic teaching.

An Early Start for your Child with Autism: Using Everyday Activities to Help Kids Connect, Communicate, and Learn by Sally J. Rogers, Ph.D., Geraldine Dawson, Ph.D., and Laurie A. Vismara, Ph.D. – This book is based on the evidence-based, breakthrough program Early Start Denver Model (ESDM). It has numerous, easy-to-implement, practical strategies that can be used daily to promote a child's crucial developmental skills.

❄ *Clay's Story*, **Pages 8-9:** Peer training packages and modeling are both evidence-based practices. Relationships between children who are typically developing and children on the autism spectrum enhance the lives of both. Most children gain empathy, patience, and a sense of self-worth from these friendships. The development of these special relationships can significantly help to prevent bullying. Typically developing children provide language and social models. Children with ASD learn crucial social skills from being in an environment where the teacher, parent, and therapist purposefully create and use social situations to model and teach social skills. One can set up a playgroup or enroll a child in a social skills group that targets specific skills, such as taking turns and initiating play. Teachers of inclusive classrooms have the wonderful opportunity of social teaching possibilities throughout the day.

It is important to note that not all children with ASD will benefit from full inclusion. The full inclusion classroom can be overstimulating and overwhelming for a child with significant sensory needs and developmental delays. More progress can be made with these children in a smaller, less-stimulating, and more individualized environment, using increased time in the inclusive environment as the child is able to handle. Every child is unique, and great care must be taken to provide the child with the learning environment that best meets his or her needs.

www.specialneeds.thebullyproject.com – This website has specially designed toolkits for parents, teachers, and students dealing with bullying and children with special needs.

www.herointhehall.com – This website focuses on teaching and empowering bystanders to speak up against bullying. Resources are available for entire schools, parents, and students.

www.modelmekids.com – This website offers videos that feature modeling of important social skills.

www.inclusivechildcare.net – This website has many resources to help promote successful, inclusive programming for young children. It includes an online consultation service to support providers in keeping children with challenging behaviors or special needs in child care programs.

❈ *Clay's Story*, **Page 10:** The "Premack Principle" (Grandma's rule – first, eat your vegetables, then you can have dessert) is a very effective behavioral tool. It is used to motivate a child to complete a less-preferred task to have access to a reinforcer, i.e., "First, do this work, and then you get to choose."

❈ *Clay's Story*, **Page 11:** All young children need many experiences with different fine motor activities to build hand strength and coordination. Children with developmental delays and SPD often avoid such activities, resulting in increased delays in hand development, self-help skills, and writing skills. Geoboards, pegboards, lacing, stringing beads, puzzles, eyedroppers, pop beads, play dough, Thera-Putty©, and writing in sand are all simple activities to enhance hand development. Changing these activities often helps to keep the child's interest. To help a child develop a tripod grasp, break a crayon into one-inch pieces. A child will be forced to use the correct grasp. Have the child write on a vertical board or on a slanted surface to develop wrist strength. Have a child hold a pom pom against his palm with the pinky and ring finger and hold their writing utensil with a tripod grasp. Put a thin layer of sand or salt in a tray or a cookie sheet and have the child practice writing shapes and letters with their fingers. This is a good exercise to help a child become less sensory defensive. The child may need an occupational therapy evaluation to determine specific fine motor and sensory needs.

www.prekinders.com/fine-motor-skills/ - Visit this website for creative, thematic, fine motor activities.

www.hwtears.com/hwt – "Handwriting Without Tears®" is a multisensory handwriting program. This program has many materials that make it fun to learn the formation of letters, and it appeals to various types of learning styles.

www.letterschool.com – This is an inexpensive application to teach formation and recognition of letters and numbers. It also teaches recognition of letter sounds.

www.montessori-n-such.com – This site has many unique fine motor activities and materials.

www.otplan.com – A search can be made for fine motor activities by available materials or by skills that need to be strengthened.

✿ *Clay's Story*, Page 12: All young children, especially children with ASD, need help in learning how to self-regulate their emotional and physiological states. Dr. Becky Bailey created the concept of a "Safe Place" to aid in this process. The Conscious Discipline website offers specific materials to be used in a "Safe Place." Setting up a "Safe Place" in the classroom or home can provide a child with a place that is safe to go when they are overwhelmed emotionally or when their sensory systems are overloaded. Children can be taught about emotions by using pictures of children experiencing different emotions that they can identify with or recognize. Children can be taught different calming techniques that they can use when they feel overwhelmed. Sensory items can be made available for the child to choose. Providing a "Safe Place" where an overwhelmed child can go helps to reduce outbursts in the classroom and at home.

www.consciousdiscipline.com – Visit this website for free visuals to print and post in the "Safe Place" to help a child learn to self-calm. Available for purchase are a "Feelings Buddies Self-Regulation Tool Kit" and an "I Choose: Self-Control Board." One can also find information about upcoming dates for Conscious Discipline Workshops and Summer Institutes.

Creating the School Family, Bully Proofing your School Through Emotional Intelligence by Dr. Becky Bailey – This book has detailed information on setting up a "Safe Place" and teaching children self-calming techniques. The book contains other activities to build a sense of community and social connectedness in the classroom. ***Managing Emotional Mayhem*** by Dr. Becky Bailey – This book teaches adults new skills, so that they can teach children self-regulation skills.

❊ *Clay's Story*, Page 13: Children who do not have a functional means of communicating their wants and needs will usually engage in problem behaviors in an attempt to get their needs met. Teaching a child to mand, or request, what they want can serve to greatly reduce negative behaviors. Many communication and behavioral applications now exist that can help to open the door of communication for these children. These applications can be easily integrated into a child's day from a smartphone or tablet.

The Verbal Behavior Approach: How to Teach children with Autism and Related Disorders by Mary Lynch Barbera.

www.autismapps.wikispaces.com – This website has behavioral and communication applications.

www.autism-society.org – Autism Society of America is a grassroots organization that provides current information regarding treatment, education, research, and advocacy. A helpful resource locater is available by state. If your child is impacted by the DSM-5 ASD diagnosis change, call the contact center of the Autism Society of America for information and help, 1-800-3-Autism (1-800-328-8476).

www.autismspeaks.org – This website offers information on early detection of autism spectrum disorder and free, informational toolkits for parents and teachers. The Autism Response Team can be reached at 888-288-4762, or en Español 888-772-9050.

www.cdc.gov/ncbddd/autism/index.html - This section of the Centers for Disease Control and Prevention (CDC) website provides information on early detection of ASD, treatment, and resources. www.cdc.gov/milestones – This section of the CDC website lists developmental milestones for children.

www.acf.hhs.gov/programs/ecd/watch-me-thrive - *Birth to 5: Watch Me Thrive*, is part of a coordinated federal effort by multiple agencies to encourage developmental and behavioral screening and support for children, families, and the providers who care for them.

www.firstsigns.org - This website is dedicated to helping families and professionals learn about the early warning signs of ASD. It has a free "ASD Video Glossary" to help recognize the early red flags of ASD.

www.projectlifesaver.org - This website provides timely response to save lives and reduce potential injury for children and adults who wander due to ASD, Alzheimer's, etc. A person prone to wandering can be enrolled in the program.

www.unicornchildrensfoundation.org - Unicorn Children's Foundation is an international, non-profit organization dedicated to education, leadership, and funding of innovative programs that ensure the success and inclusion of neurodiverse individuals.

www.casaforchildren.org - Did you know that an abused or neglected child with a Court Appointed Special Advocate (CASA) volunteer is more likely to find a safe and permanent home? Melissa has served as a CASA volunteer for over 10 years. If you would like additional details about becoming a CASA volunteer for abused and neglected children, please look at the information available on the CASA website.

SUMMARY

Early identification of autism spectrum disorder is crucial in helping children to receive the early intervention they will need to reach their maximum potential. Evidence-based research repeatedly proves that intensive early intervention is one of the main keys in helping children with ASD to reach their full capacity. It is my hope that this book has furnished practical, easy-to-understand strategies to help your child or your students achieve all they possibly can. Please accept each child as the truly unique individual that he or she is. Each child will develop in his own time and in his own special way. I urge you to treasure every moment and not to waste precious time in denial of a child's sensory, social, and learning needs. You can start applying these simple strategies right now.

❅ ❅ ❅

REFERENCES

American Psychiatric Association. (2013). *Diagnostic and Statistical Manual of Mental Disorders, 5th Edition: DSM-5.* Arlington, VA: American Psychiatric Publishing.

Bailey, B. A. (2000/2001). *Conscious Discipline.* Oviedo, FL: Loving Guidance, Inc.

Bailey, B. A. (2011). *Creating the School Family: Bully-Proofing Schools Through Emotional Intelligence.* Oviedo, FL: Loving Guidance, Inc.

Centers for Disease Control and Prevention (CDC). (2014). "Prevalence of Autism Spectrum Disorder Among Children Aged 8 Years—Autism and Developmental Disabilities Monitoring Network, 11 Sites, United States, 2010." *Surveillance Summaries*, March 28, 2014/63(SS02);1-21.

Grandin, Temple. (2006/2010). *Thinking in Pictures, Expanded Edition: My Life with Autism.* New York, NY: Vintage Books, A Division of Random House, Inc.

Gray, Carol. (1994/2000). *The New Social Story Book.* Arlington, TX: Future Horizons, Inc.

Greenspan, Stanley and Salmon, Jacqueline. (1996). *The Challenging Child: Understanding, Raising and Enjoying the Five Types of Children.* Cambridge, MA: Perseus Books.

Kranowitz, Carol. (2005). *The Out of Sync Child: Recognizing and Coping with Sensory Processing Disorder.* New York, NY: Penguin Group (USA), Inc.

National Autism Center. (2011). *National Autism Center's A Parent's Guide to Evidence-Based Practice and Autism.* Randolph, MA: National Autism Center.

National Autism Center. (2011). *National Autism Center's Evidence-Based Practice and Autism in the Schools.* Randolph, MA: National Autism Center.

Rogers, Sally J., Dawson, Geraldine, and Vismara, Laurie, A. (2012). *An Early Start for your Child with Autism.* New York, NY: Guilford Press.